SOLVING SCIENCE MYSTERIES

Why Does Thunder Clap?

All About Weather

Michael McMahon

PowerKiDS press™

New York

Published in 2010 by The Rosen Publishing Group, Inc.
29 East 21st Street, New York, NY 10010

Produced and designed by Denise Ryan & Associates
Editors: Helen Moore and Edwina Hamilton
Designer: Anita Adams
Photographer: Lyz Turner-Clark
U.S. Editor: Kara Murray

Photo Credits: pp. 5 top and second from top, 16 top, 17, 19 and 23: Photolibrary; p. 5 third from top: Copyright University Corporation for Atmospheric Research, Photo by Carlye Calvin; p. 5 circle: Chris Chidsey; p. 5 bottom: Donald Gruener; p. 6 bottom: Bureau of Meteorology; p. 7 top: © Photographer: Richard Thompson | Agency: Dreamstime.com; p. 8 bottom: Bonnie Schupp; p. 9 bottom: NOAA; p. 11 top: Clint Spencer; p. 11 bottom: Nellie Buir; p. 12 top left: William Picard; p. 12 top middle: © Photographer: Sonja Foos | Agency: Dreamstime.com; p. 12 centre: Nick Schlax; p. 12 bottom left: Science Photo Library; p. 13 top: Henk Badenhorst; pp. 13 and 15 bottom: NASA; p. 14 top: Christopher Bruno; p 15 top: Brian Plonka, Spokesman Review, courtesy World Picture News; p. 18 left: Miles Sherrill.

Library of Congress Cataloging-in-Publication Data

McMahon, Michael.
  Why does thunder clap? : all about weather / Michael McMahon.
    p. cm. — (Solving science mysteries)
  Includes index.
  ISBN 978-1-4488-0406-1 (library binding) — ISBN 978-1-4488-0407-8 (pbk.) —
ISBN 978-1-4488-0408-5 (6-pack)
  1. Weather—Juvenile literature. I. Title.
  QC981.3.M46 2010
  551.6—dc22

2009038280

Manufactured in the United States of America

CPSIA Compliance Information: Batch #WW10PK: For Further Information contact Rosen Publishing, New York, New York at 1-800-237-9932

Contents

Questions About Weather

Q: What Causes Earth's weather?

A: The Sun provides the **energy** that causes Earth's weather. It heats the air in various parts of Earth's atmosphere by different amounts. This causes masses of warm and cold air to move from place to place, creating winds. The winds bring sunny, wet, or stormy weather. When we talk about weather, we mean the state of Earth's atmosphere at a particular time and place. Weather reports include the temperature and if it is wet and windy or dry and calm.

Q: What causes wind?

A: Winds are caused by the Sun heating air masses unevenly in different parts of the world. Air that is warmed by the Sun becomes lighter and rises. This creates an area of low pressure where there is less air pressing down on Earth. Because air always flows from an area of high pressure to an area of low pressure, cooler air flows in to fill the space left by the rising air. A light breeze springs up when the air moves slowly. Gales and **hurricanes** tear through the skies when the air moves very quickly.

Q: Do different winds bring different kinds of weather?

A: The direction of the wind can tell you a lot about what weather to expect. Different winds bring the influence of different air masses with them. Air masses above **continents** are dry, those above the sea are moist, tropical air masses are warm, and polar air masses are cold. Some winds bring sunny weather and others bring rain, snow, and mist. In North America, winds from the north bring cold weather and winds from the west bring rain.

weather map

Q: How do we know what weather is coming our way?

A: Meteorologists gather information about the weather from satellites, balloons, barometers, and other instruments. These scientists use computers to help them analyze the data that they have gained. Meteorologists then use the information to create weather maps for us to read. Weather maps show the weather at any one time or they forecast the weather coming our way. The maps have symbols to show weather conditions such as rainfall and wind direction.

Coriolis Effect
Earth's rotation turns winds to the right in the Northern Hemisphere and to the left in the Southern Hemisphere. This is called the Coriolis effect after the French physics professor Gaspard-Gustave de Coriolis (1792–1843), who first showed that winds moving across a spinning surface follow a curved path.

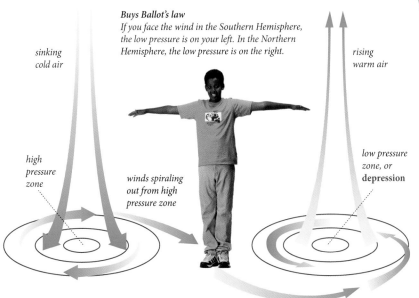

sinking cold air

Buys Ballot's law
If you face the wind in the Southern Hemisphere, the low pressure is on your left. In the Northern Hemisphere, the low pressure is on the right.

rising warm air

high pressure zone

winds spiraling out from high pressure zone

low pressure zone, or **depression**

winds spiraling into a low pressure zone

Questions About Clouds

Q: How are clouds formed?

A: Clouds are formed by rising air. Air becomes cooler as it rises and becomes less and less able to hold invisible **water vapor**. There comes a point—called dew point—at which the air becomes so cold that the water vapor condenses to form tiny droplets of water. Sometimes even ice crystals form.

altostratus clouds

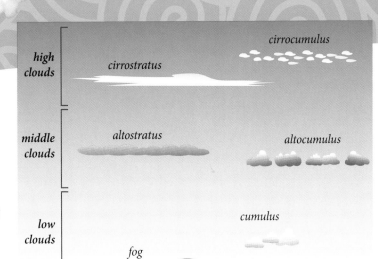

types of clouds

high clouds

cirrostratus

cirrocumulus

middle clouds

altostratus

altocumulus

low clouds

cumulus

fog

Q: Why are some clouds so dark?

A: The clouds that contain the most water are the darkest. The water in these **dense** clouds blocks the Sun from view. Dark, gray clouds are the ones that are most likely to bring rain.

cumulus clouds

Q: Why are clouds different shapes?

A: The shape of clouds depends upon the way they form. It also depends upon the balance of water droplets and ice crystals in them. Sometimes air rises rapidly over a small area to form small, puffy clouds, called cumulus, which rarely last for more than a few hours. At other times, air can rise slowly over a wide area to form vast, shapeless clouds, called stratus, which cover the entire sky and last for days.

Questions About Thunder and Lightning

Q: Why does thunder clap?

A: Thunder occurs when lightning races through the air. A flash of lightning heats the air along its path so dramatically that it expands at supersonic speed. This expansion causes a deafening clap of thunder.

Q: Why does lightning strike?

A: When cloud particles become electrically charged by bumping into each other, positively charged particles collect at the top of the cloud, while negatively charged particles stay at the bottom. Once a big difference in charge builds up, sheet lightning flashes between the two to cancel it out. Often lightning does not discharge between the clouds but toward the positively charged ground. This creates dramatic forks of lightning.

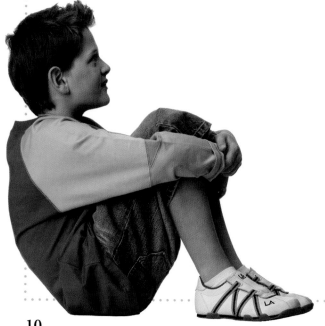

the vortex of a tornado

Q: What is a tornado?

A: Tornadoes start deep within vast thunderclouds where a column of rising warm air is set spinning by high winds roaring through the top of the cloud. As this spinning **vortex** becomes stronger, it comes down through the cloud base, whirling violently and sucking up everything in its path. Tornadoes, which often occur in the Midwest, can cause an enormous amount of damage to crops, buildings, and other structures.

forked lightning

It's a Fact

> The Deadliest Tornado

The deadliest single tornado in U.S. history was the Tristate Tornado of March 18, 1925, which killed 695 people. It was on the ground continuously for 219 miles (352 km) as it raced across southeastern Missouri, southern Illinois, and southwestern Indiana in about 3 ½ hours.

> The Hottest Day

The highest temperature ever recorded in the United States was reached on July 5, 1913, when the mercury soared to 134° F (57° C) in Death Valley, California.

> The Coldest Temperature

The coldest temperature in North America was recorded on February 3, 1947, in Snag, Canada, when it dipped to −81.4° F (−63° C). Snag's climate is like that of Siberia, one of the coldest places on Earth.

> Ice Storm

In December 2007, a devastating ice storm swept across the central United States. At least 15 people were killed and 1-inch-(2.5 cm) thick ice coated parts of Oklahoma and Missouri. More than 600,000 homes and businesses were left without electricity after icy winds brought down power lines and trees.

> A World Record Wave

On September 11, 1995, the *QE2* ocean liner was struck by a 98-foot (30 m) wave during Hurricane Luis off the coast of Newfoundland, Canada. The wave is the largest wave ever measured.

> Waterspouts

When rotating columns of air similar to tornadoes occur over water, the tremendous power of the upward draft causes a sucking action that draws up the water and creates a waterspout. They are not very dangerous but they are spectacular to see.

> That's Rain!

The most intense rainfall ever recorded was on November 26, 1970, in Barst, on the Caribbean island of Guadeloupe, where 1.5 inches (38.1 mm) fell in just 1 minute!

the eye of a hurricane

> Hurricane Katrina

Hurricane Katrina was one of the most powerful and damaging hurricanes ever to hit the United States. The hurricane hit southern Florida on August 25, 2005, and on August 29, it slammed the Gulf Coast with 127-mile-per-hour (204 km/h) winds and huge storm surges, which caused massive flooding in New Orleans. At least 1,800 people were killed, 1,464 of those deaths occurred in Louisiana.

Can You Believe It?

Blue Skies

The sky appears to be blue because of the way light from the Sun is **reflected** off gas molecules in the air. Dust, water droplets, and other particles **dilute** the intensity of the blue by reflecting other colors so the skies are bluest when the air is at its purest.

Rainbow colors

Rainbows are the reflection of the Sun in raindrops, which is why they appear after sudden showers and why they are always seen opposite the Sun. The colors come from the way the raindrops split the sunlight into a **spectrum** of colors. Because the sunlight catches each raindrop at a different angle, we see a different part of the spectrum reflected in each drop. Rainbow colors always appear in the same order: red, orange, yellow, green, blue, **indigo**, and violet.

> In June 2006, the frigid sky above the Idaho plains was lit in a brilliant spectrum of color. The Sun shone through ice crystals in a high-level cloud, creating the rare meteorological event known as a circumhorizon arc.

< This is an orbiting spacecraft like the one that took the photograph below.

Hurricane Tracking

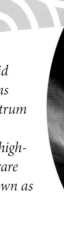

Photographs taken in space are used to track hurricanes and predict their paths. Important information is also gained from special aircraft that fly into the middle or eye of the hurricane. These aircraft measure the size and strength of the storm. In addition, radio signals about what is happening with the wind and the water are sent from weather ships and **buoys** to hurricane-tracking centers.

Who found out?

Air Pressure: Evangelista Torricelli

Evangelista Torricelli (1608–1647), an Italian scientist, was the first to discover the existence of air pressure. To find out why water could never be pumped up more than 33 feet (10 m), Torricelli filled a 3-foot (1 m) glass tube with the heaviest liquid—**mercury**. He then turned it upside down and held the open end under the surface of a bowl of mercury. The mercury in the tube dropped to about 30 inches (76 cm), leaving a vacuum in the top of the tube. Torricelli concluded that it was the pressure of the atmosphere on the surface of the mercury in the bowl that prevented the mercury in the tube from falling any farther.

Wind Strength: Sir Francis Beaufort

The first system for comparing wind strength was the Beaufort scale, which was devised by the English admiral Sir Francis Beaufort (1774–1857) in 1806. Beaufort realized that a simple way to judge wind strengths was to compare the way sailing ships must be rigged in different winds. His scale had 13 wind strengths, with calm as Force 0 and a hurricane at Force 12. The scale, which is still often used today, was later adapted for use on land, using indicators such as rising smoke, breaking trees, and falling chimneys.

The True Nature of Lightning: Benjamin Franklin

The American statesman and scientist Benjamin Franklin (1706–1790) discovered the true nature of lightning. Franklin thought lightning might be electricity. Electricity was little understood at that time, but scientists had figured out how to create static electricity. To test his idea, Franklin flew a kite during a thunderstorm. A metal key was attached to the kite string by a thread. Electricity from the clouds flowed down the wet string to the key. When Franklin put his hand near the key, he felt a mild electric shock and saw sparks like those created by static electricity generators. He had proved his point but he was lucky to be alive.

Weather Forecasting:
Lewis Richardson

English meteorologist Lewis Richardson (1881–1953) believed that the best way to forecast weather was to take a wide range of observations at the same time from evenly spaced points throughout the world. By doing this, an accurate forecast could be made. Richardson tried to use an early calculator to do the many calculations required but it was not suitable for the task. Now that supercomputers have been developed, numerical forecasting, which was Richardson's idea, has become a reality.

It's Quiz Time!

The pages where you can find the answers are shown in the red circles, except where otherwise noted.

Find the odd one out

1. cumulus clouds   stratus clouds   ⑨

   cirrus clouds   thick clouds

2. Benjamin Franklin   Katrina   ⑬

   Gaspard Coriolis   Evangelista Torricelli

3. atmosphere   water spouts   ④

   tornadoes   hurricanes

Choose the correct words

1. Without the (Sun, Moon, Venus) we would not only be very cold, we would also have no weather at all. ④

2. Winds are caused by the Sun heating (ice crystals, land, air masses) unevenly in different parts of the world. ⑤

3. The colors of the rainbow always appear in the same order (red, orange, silver, yellow, crimson, green, blue, purple, indigo, gold, and violet). ⑭

Complete these sentences

1. Thunder is made by lightning as it scorches through
   __ __ __   __ __ __ . ⑩

2. Clouds are formed by __ __ __ __ __ __   __ __ __ . ⑧

3. Scientists known as __ __ __ __ __ __ __ __ __ __ __ __ __
   gather information about the weather from satellites, balloons, and
   other instruments. ⑦

4. Tornadoes can cause an enormous amount of __ __ __ __ __ __
   to crops, buildings, and other structures. ⑪

Try It out

Go back and read about why the sky looks blue on page 14. We are going to see how it works firsthand.

What You'll Need

- a large soda bottle with the label removed, a flashlight, a few thick books, milk, and water

1 Fill the soda bottle about three-quarters of the way with water. Use the books to rest your flashlight on its side, so it can shine through the side of the bottle. What color is the light?

2

Add a spoonful of milk to the water in the bottle, put the cap on, and shake it. Keep adding milk until the light starts to look blue. The milk in the bottle acts like the dust and other particles in the atmosphere.

Glossary

buoys (BOO-eez) Anchored floating objects.

continents (KON-tuh-nents) Large, unbroken landmasses, such as North America, Europe, and Australia.

dense (DENTS) Thickly, closely packed.

depression (dih-PREH-shun) An area of low pressure into which strong winds blow counter-clockwise in the Northern Hemisphere and clockwise in the Southern Hemisphere.

dilute (dy-LOOT) To make weaker.

energy (EH-ner-jee) Usable power such as heat or electricity.

hurricanes (HUR-ih-kaynz) Storms with strong winds of at least 75 miles per hour (120 km/h).

indigo (IN-dih-goh) A dark purplish blue color.

lightning (LYT-ning) A brilliant flash of light in the sky caused by the release of natural electricity in the air during a thunderstorm.

mercury (MER-kyuh-ree) A liquid metal used in thermometers.

particles (PAR-tih-kulz) Very small pieces.

reflected (rih-FLEKT-ed) Thrown or cast back from a surface.

spectrum (SPEK-trum) The series of bands produced when white light is split into seven colors.

vortex (VOR-teks) A whirling mass of air.

water vapor (WAH-ter VAY-pur) Gaseous water.

Index

Web Sites

Due to the changing nature of Internet links, PowerKids Press has developed an online list of Web sites related to the subject of this book. This site is updated regularly. Please use this link to access the list:

www.powerkidslinks.com/ssm/clap/